The man behind the hands:
I GOTCHA NUMBER

BY
JoeL Washington-Atterberry

Contact Information

Email: atterberry71@icloud.com

Website: www.mrjoelharris1430.com

Facebook: Joel washington atterberry

Instagram: king_atterberry7

Instagram: mentallity9

Copyrighted © 2020 Library of Congress
ISBN: 978-0-578-23425-0

Published by King atterberry 9

Artwork by: Christine jones

Preface

During this time of the pandemic, the guard has chosen to bring forth more writing into existence of showing growth through my enlightenment of truth.

Creating a wave of poetry through elevation and evolution as a narrator of the true and living.

As a healthcare worker in this field of 19 years I have been the eyes and ears of the nurses, being schooled by a multitude of nurses helped me understand my position as a certified medication aide.

I have written my other books under the moniker names of Joel Harris and king atterberry THE GUARD.

Everything is energy vibes and frequency within my will to exhibit my creativity in an artistic form.

Take a walk down the road of the mind of a Harlem author and poet that reside at the shore of cape may, new jersey.

This book is dedicated to my cousin Brian Johnson,

family first.

love comes in all shapes, sizes to form.

Much love to you CUZO I'm here!!

Table of Contents

Send them out

Yawl man broads be acting too masculine you feminine.

Colorful like m&ms better call who ever sent you in.

Notice of a recall reject to where the real at.

Peeped out your sad act I was born on third rail tracks.

Hug pound the dawgs yeah, we walk on the concrete.

Back home I am bare feet waiting for a bite to eat.

Some talking hating I check on my family.

Offset the fantasy my strength be reality.

Stay inside the realm that is held by the creator.

Blessings well provided my hands touch the paper.

Whether minor or major the outlook in my favor.

Crawl before you walk and stand tall like skyscrapers.

Come on yawl

Yeah bring me all the smoke fire up the booth light the track up.

I am about to act up cut loose the chains release the factors.

Big boy the tractor trailer moving on you small lames.

Rolling on this lane it is doctor strange setting off things.

Demonstrating upper eighties rap skills my pen ill.

No matter how you feel my strong will give your bars chills.

Meditate remain still no emotion signal out to those.

Capturing a goat soul and essence break the dirt mold.

Show your hands and fold through poems you been shown.

From the lines designed on the page you see how the guard grown.

No mystery just his story nobody else move ink for me.

From the home of the spitters this that NYC poetry.

You ever wonder!

Got to see the highlights between the high lights in ceilings.

As a youth when your praying while kneeling killing your demons.

Manifesting what you question and answer while in silence.

Exonerate your violence with thoughtfulness and kindness.

What you see is what you get from the prospective of an author.

Be careful drinking water from that cup inside the saucer.

Is it from where it is supposed to be speaking to freely?

If society stop and read a couple of pages from king atterberry.

Instagram a post not doing the most just checking in.

Calling on family and friends let us send a memo and pretend.

Mind closed third eye open to the next book coming.

While my age group is sleeping, I am hungry eating something.

Lots of food for thought accept knowledge being fed.

Only teachings are not dead it is resurrected from a pledge.

Take away the timeline and the features that it has.

No vessels will crash enjoying moments just to laugh.

Original

Pick him up that is what the others say when a hand is needed.

It is not hard to reach it peep it band together treat it.

Pray upon the ailments though the moments keep failing.

What is known they keep bailing cause they methods are upscaling.

Some die in the culture while the civilized wonder why.

Through my eyes from the sky was created by my high.

Left earth returned home entered another zone.

Meditating with crystals and stones creating my own **xylophone.

Days off alone or spin clock a friend and win.

Cycle a blend of trends that mend ways of a Washington.

Bathe in the light of the source my retrospective thoughts.

Camouflage Muhammad notes and quotes holding a force.

Signs of the rhyme

Back to the pedigree moving along inside of space.

My heart race got to control the natural pace.

What appear in this universe is a paradox of elements.

Adjusting my etiquette, a requirement when I am settling.

Walk around stop stand my ground at destinations.

Elevating my patience never know what you are facing.

Always a believer the benevolent has bestowed.

Weight of a lifetime living ease your mind body soul.

Half-truths be told play your role on the dice rolled.

Headed to the plateau the grass is scarce on the road.

Application for peace submitted far and beyond.

Heard the music to a song and wrote this right off the arm.

Line of mine

When I become a giant soon walk with the tyrants.

Witness my deviance when I join the alliance.

My peoples dropping science hearing all that is sincere.

Damn right I appear close and near never to fear.

Bear witness to an atterberry king from southern land.

Surrounded by marsh sand building with sons of man.

Some only get a glance of the real and just be talking.

But frankly when I am speaking conversations be important.

Play a course on a Tee who be free on lost days.

The guard be on his way you see me post about the bay.

Rise above the bullshit displayed by the mannequin.

My pen is a lightsaber defeating the dark Anakin.

Possessed by the dark side pull poems out my archive.

They better run and hide cause any moment can be do or die.

I came a long way to being who I have become.

Shining like the sun Harlem world is where I am from.

Where you at yo? Part.2

Amazing is the piece that I release some can keep.

This verse is just a treat in which I give outside my peace.

Food for thought never bought only revive what was lost.

Knowledge can be free and at the same time cost.

Information traded haters hate it we going to make it.

Bring back the essence of favorites therefore nothing is outdated.

Grieve for the teachers who been misplaced in history.

Say a prayer for the speakers that expose hidden mystery.

Restore what has been abandoned to be destroyed in the future.

Do not let the devils fool ya they are mental mind intruders.

Manipulating maneuvers directing falsified news.

Execute your power now and do not lose your sight of view.

Higher than

Fly inside the booth shake a leg adjust my bread.

Pockets with no change call up a chick for some head.

Beautiful women lay my luxury ways upon them.

Place my atterberry love in they necessary forum.

Log in stay in do no matter heavy or slim.

She can be a distant or close fair weather friend.

Her ways start to spin send her heart affection.

Call me Mr. Washington if my Harris name end.

My smile gives them feelings as if born in fifty-two.

Spirit of man born in thirty-two I am coming through.

Nice guy on the landing site I come down from a different height.

Blind hoes with my delight of having an appetite.

E.O.TO (each one teaches one)

Ayo, I grew in the culture where you were when I remember.

After I gained knowledge of self, I bounced ninety-two December.

Real shit that army bag was on my shoulder with a backpack.

Pen and pencils with raps and nice tracks it is all facts.

So, years later I returned to the apple because I had to.

Resurrect my lifestyle and bring fruition of my truth.

Bagged bitches that was loose under my arm like a noose.

Built in ciphers with my cousins and our enlightener was not fooled.

Traveled around the city learning and speaking in a tongue.

Back then I was young in my twenties a rising sun.

My spirituality was beyond a dimension I kept disclosed.

If brothers show and prove, then I would have time and grow.

Out the gate

When I knock it out the park people no remarks?

If it is really gone time let me light up the dark.

Walk across bridges enter tunnels no life.

If Joel is Jehovah I am not related to Christ.

My spirit shine bright working a graveyard shift.

Maybe speak to the sith as if I hold it hostage.

Hands blessed properly when I work on properties.

Respect THE GUARD honesty soon writers honor me.

Yawl peeped out the seven I got new projects coming.

Thoughts be in my head as my wheels keep running.

Officially and socially learning I am on time with it.

whole world mirage and facade keeping the people distant.

Guard Up! (Masked dimension)

Throw your goon in a dope feign and unarm his hands.

Smack the shit out your man spit in the face of your fans.

Now that a brother is out of character this scene is mastered.

Here is what you see and hear a whole bunch of laughter.

Settle it old school slap box or throw hands in the street.

Alleviate the heat, knuckle up and wake the concrete.

Something got to give when you talk that stupid shit.

Get kicked in your ass punched in your face splitting your lips.

Eye jammies delivered maybe your sight need a wake up.

Stop being a sucker and a hater turned traitor.

Loyalty is in question it is obvious you cannot stand up.

Walking with sagging trousers you need to pull your pants up.

Man be a man stop fronting this cannot be life bro.

Let that bullshit go unless you need time to grow.

Keep it a buck fifty on the real take it off the reel.

OGS know the deal and how it feels let us spin the wheel.

Make your own line!!

Do not rob the next man or woman of creativity.

Come on just leave it be especially if styling free.

What emerge was not heard but a last-minute verse.

Un-rehearsed inside is worth a loud applause on the work.

Waiting in the wing for someone to do they think.

Walk in someone else's shoes and lace up the damn strings.

I believe in what is right igniting different poetry.

There is nobody holding or folding THE GUARD telepathy.

Sending out a memo from a mental killing the nonsense.

Go ahead and spill the content and face a new comment.

True form galaxian born inside Manhattan.

Experience what is happening when we expose the acting.

Up next

The god said move accordingly that is what time I am on.

Remain strong do not get torn I am only just getting warm.

It is gone ahead and lift the world up peel back the layers.

Treat different states with flavors and make green paper.

Hit my barber get my sides tapered do not touch the beard.

My strength of a seer bares the knowledge that I wear.

King Atterberry check the crown with the nine-emblem shining.

At my age I am still rhyming because my skill set remind them.

That is the new dudes rapping Ayo bro what is happening.

Yawl style got me laughing where the hip-hop passion is.

Leave my prints on tracks if I am featured on a track.

It is my third rail flow letting me bring it all back.

New York flyer

These brothers are ducks in the pond and cannot bear arms.

Thought they was the bomb until they met GALLOTRON.

Movement for real I am the antidote for tracks.

Some will not ever get it back because they rap is whack.

Lace up my boots with a military mindset.

Have no regrets when I fly pass your set.

What else can you expect from a healthcare vet.

Nineteen staying off the guillotine I am Star Trek.

Moving at mock five against the lying eyes.

Whenever THE GUARD arrive element of surprise.

Wipe away your tears maybe crack a few beers.

I am that Washington atterberry reconnecting peers.

I used to work on a boat that was docked at a pier.

Left that old atmosphere and found another career.

That was ninety-two excused me from the floating.

Moms passed took a southern path on greyhound smoking.

By myself!!

When I am in a cool mood, I am running dropping smooth jewels.

Later for these weak dudes that want to be cruel.

Watch how I act up stepping outside my character.

Defending my own principles Starbuck of Galactica.

Word to dirk Benedict I am more face man with an A-team.

Staying on track let me find my future in my cold dreams.

Warm calm and pleasant do not prejudge my stature.

All black writers matter so excuse my manners.

Notebooks in my backpack also fellow authors books.

Bars delivered written with intent no need for hooks.

Capture many moments what I say and do I own it.

Think outside the box search the world for components.

I AM HE!

My old steps were yesterday's news for all you sucker.

I banded with some brothers' sharper than leave cutters.

Mark points on subject matter what happened to yawl opinion.

Get out your damn feeling and adjust your standard living.

Now that I am resilient building blocks on social media.

Perhaps the fake fevers can be washed 2000 lever.

Go getters unite join forces turn life around.

Traveling different grounds speaking across many sounds.

If I jumped out my own skin and twin my best friend.

Loyalty begin once again seeing a dead end.

Grab my old soul write a book called ole joel.

Another creative body of work that show my goals.

Stories forever told on how I master my own craft.

Sitting in a bubble bath to relax bust out and laugh.

Yea I did it again prize fighting like a boxer.

New jack city watcher who also love the movie clockers.

Out the window

Days begin in the morning after the shower and my clothes on.

Moving right along get in my car and play songs.

Got a place that I go to when I clear my mental thoughts.

Yesterday I saw more troubled souls than before.

So, my prayers become enhanced and meditations deeper.

As I awake open my consciousness to tunes by singing speakers.

Vibes be alive as I relax to what I am hearing.

Return to my vehicle and drive away steering.

Place my energy inside a destination where I am headed to.

Nice eatery where I lunch and get a mouthful.

Do a little reading drinking coffee as my beverage.

They know me by three letters spelled out to measure.

JWA or the writer king atterberry.

I keep some places private as if it was my sanctuary.

Love to write on life possibilities and honesty.

While those who make fun, I know others are fond of me.

Never know waves

It is the man behind the hands with ide and illekes.

Yoruba culture displayed blessed in Africa always.

Never copped from a gift shop blessed inside a temple.

Rehearsing my best lines for my cd on my kindle.

Study Hindi and other spiritual parts in religions.

My past life beginning once again when I am remembering.

Who and what I was channel feelings on some dope tracks?

Whoever thought I fell off my pops spirit strikes back.

Grab your attention when I mention my ascension.

Born in a dimension where I am living just chilling.

The odyssey of me is just an imagery of leaves.

Grab a hold of what you seek everyone you cannot please.

OVER-TIME

I am only five nine when I was forty-five and thirty-six.

Things was built became damaged and lost in conflict.

Even at twenty-seven the hardest lesson was a blessing.

During the courts operational session held back confessions.

Turn of events that went left gave mouth to mouth.

Kept alive the house but my lifestyle changed routes.

Stepped in a lane that I remembered back in my teens.

At eighteen became a writing machine studio feign.

By the age of fifty-four behind a door I will flip a score.

May the future help me soar to a place that is unexplored?

It is something else

We used to dream as a youth for bigger and better ways of living.

Collateral damage by world leaders toward the people giving.

Strong assistance brilliant, we skilled inside our practice.

But on the tv the news reporters are actors and actresses.

A lot of things scripted while families absorb the lies.

Watch the crocodile tears run down faces with fake cries.

What we once knew before does not exist anymore.

Government system changing laws we feel the last straw.

No win loses or draw things are real out in the field.

What was concealed is now revealed we need a spiritual shield.

Groups of people praying, lots of others suffering.

Be mindful what you trust and be-careful who you are loving.

Who you!!

Bring a force within nature allow the universe to post up!

Anything the man behind the hands touch is closer.

My roundabout way of feeling good is to see.

New improved reflection that connect all possibilities.

Emotions are not tied but I keep my lids open.

Being vocal and focused on portals obtaining tokens.

Find a cloud that mirror any thought that make sense.

Lock it in my mental Rolodex until it is made evidence.

The guard do not lie I lost many to the skies.

When the memories rise from underneath embrace the high.

Start a wave of reading different like I am back at study hall.

There is no win lose or draw if you keep a total recall.

Rest easy

Finally, you see what The Guard bring to life.

End your dark days with a light that shine bright.

Enough is enough I do not trust the bluff stuff.

For all you loud mouths talking I score in the clutch.

Your free throws all rim Patrick Ewing on the line.

Cindy Lauper cheerleaders time after time.

Never drop dimes pockets folded with green.

I am straight from the assist shots made with the team.

Drink the brown not the clear too many thoughts in the air.

Why stop look and stare be prepared when I am near.

Some go too far as if a star course was lost.

Heads or tails I still prevail word my arm with the cross.

Let it all be

The guard king atterberry stay spitting while yawl different.

Bars heavy cannot lift it I am distant when I visit.

Change how I look inside the here and now I switch styles.

Go ahead and talk loudly what you are saying is more in doubt.

I bounce to surroundings keep my peace well protected.

That is why some be guessing asking questions about my blessings.

Hands move words on pads without the writer's block.

Gifted from the creator and born to never want to stop.

Raised by the elders of the past I miss the draft.

Found another course no court days I map paths.

Speak to my ancestors when I pray with higher thoughts.

There is a purpose that I live for adore the unexplored.

Never worry

Just applaud the underdog and see a wave of his expression.

Any moves to destinations can be brought by a suggestion.

Awakened is the third eye been awaking my thoughts dope.

Executing one of my plans shared with others enveloped.

Dropped in a location where the clues lead you to see.

There is a message off my sleeve written down in belief.

No fabrication due to elaboration of these others.

I salute my sisters and brothers on what they may uncover.

Extension of my hand is just me do not grab an arm.

My calm will be alarmed sending vibes of what is warned.

Hear the guardian part of a squadron of authors.

Writers and reciters real appliers with much to offer.

Never that

If the virus is corona change your beer to Budweiser.

Death toll is higher let us expose the true liars.

If its manmade then create a serum call it cascade.

Clean it up fade it away and juice your body upgrade.

Vitamins and veggies hold life steady with water.

Ignore the bot callers and speak on border corners.

Fiasco of trouble that arrived and still survive.

If the cough is hard and dry, then the wheezing going to fly.

Pandemic is epic peace and blessings to all the medics.

Heard about chips being embedded somewhere yes, I read it.

Place a build on your lungs walk and talk on the reg.

The mind body and soul are not dead leave alone what is being said.

Master matter pt.1

Hurricane tenacity tornado speed on tracks.

Gallotron is back on earth living right and exact.

My demo is extracted from books that I wrote.

Send it across the globe with a nice thank you note.

Pieces of an author illustrating forms of poems.

Letting all be known how my name come out in zones.

Whether Joel Harris or king atterberry my moniker exists.

Amazon got the list social media gives me a lift.

Foundations are born some communities are warned.

Apply science to what is torn therefor we not far gone.

Guardians emerge through the times if we believe.

Study hard on degrees through an enlightener that breathe.

Antidote

Baby girl been waiting awfully long for a spark.

The guard bring a charge to her heart in near darkness.

Apart from this, we share tender sweet kisses.

Our intimate business connects from start to finish.

No pillow talks only speak on life in which we know.

Our time involved is slow connecting on levels grown.

Inside our mental thoughts we get lost within each other's.

Session of affection it is a blessing that we cover.

Fields of discovery moments in time appreciated.

Never holding expectancy, we just follow compassion greeted.

Next to me telepathy is free of who we be.

Caring for each other needs mentally and physically.

Lift me up pt.3

Step the fuck back bout to get my weight up excuse my talk I am just a brother who remember old New York.

Forget your tough talk and your weak ass thoughts, I am a genuine Jedi that hold a power source.

You think that juicing keeps me amped I do the shit others cannot.

Guided by my influential camp I am closing ramps.

Do not enter the month of April we march until the first.

My insert within my research kill off your birth.

Call up kitty when she misses me or my old school biddy.

I was Mork and she was Mindy black version in the city.

Relax with henny or Remy my memory true to form.

Enjoy writing songs or poems just know I get it on.

Promote the health wealth movement of East and west coast.

Hoping that I do not be ghost before I find another host.

Notarized

When I return as a Harris check my status through your glasses.

Through the social media mask make a mark and do damage.

Brand my own concepts inside a parallel world of living.

Some be steady drifting I unleash the dragon hidden.

Glow carry a shine from a time that keep them nervous.

Respect the full service ayo I do this with a high purpose.

Elevate the mind state create off the love and hate.

Recycle whatever despiteful people put on life's plate.

Nowadays how I play for better pay no minimum wage.

I overtime and shine and leave my bills behind decay.

Pump up like Reebok's mirror back the old swatch.

When I blow it is going to be industry hold up with knots.

Donate

Whatever words I lend you from my mental and my pencil.

On point sharp as stencils thinking quick hand on my temples.

Contemplate my thoughts on how so many blind and lost.

Still searching for the force that is kept inside the source.

My on the beach time is to clear my aura and my chakras.

Next book will be a banger that is kept from the martyrs.

The poetry I write is of a Dodge Challenger futuristic.

I am an old school dude from the manhattans stylistic.

Ok might be terrific soon I will spit it when the time come.

Big daddy on the creative side of things I get the job done.

Saluting all others that put it down and bring it out.

Is not nothing like seeing my people band together building house.

Monumental

First, my main frame adapts to change along with others.

Choice of habit let us explore the double doors of those that suffer.

History of joy and pain jump on a train that has no station stop.

Somehow, we all forgot about the people who became our rock.

Even if we band together to help from a distance.

Just like for instance prayers for hope and faith upon existence.

A handshake or a hug and a pound spread it around.

Or the words upon sound when a call is made embrace what is found.

Live love without hate create a wave of friendliness.

Block the evilness that breed in us find someone that need our trust.

Book of Joel pt.1

Hold your head for a sec take a moment to digest this.

This is early morning breakfast that will leave ladies breathless.

Catch the mindset of an author who write it and recite it.

My pen ignites a wave of books I know they like it.

Open doors in forums and platforms social media.

Come join if your eager meet a leader with the speakers.

Women yes, I greet them treat them feed them and love them.

Kiss the handles to the oven and watch them start bugging.

Send off affection bless them and caress them.

Make a brother resonate another poem without impression.

Lift up they spirit make it rise to skies of nature.

Having them calling the creator for my hands on the equator.

What is next!!

Never tardy on scheduled days of going to employment.

I know exactly where I am going a place that I do not toy wit.

See life change within a months' time in good people.

Re channel the energy of those that carry awkward evil.

Deceitful are the fools that choose to cross moving paths.

I laugh instead of giving a verbal blast of guards' math.

When they motive do not add up here is a notice of a focus.

Factors for the actors call them out for being bogus.

My embracement of spirituality will make them all heed.

What they eyes cannot see while they are living under seas.

Freeze stop them in the tracks show them a field.

Where all can be revealed and not concealed how you feel.

You know what is up

THE GUARD protect his vessel true indeed it is special.

Drive my physical forward and keeping my legs pedaled.

Summary of me some wonder where I do be.

In a place without misery so my days forever sunny.

If ever become dim interact with friends that shine.

Clowns I pay no mind they funny and pantomime.

Talking without speaking start reading and believing.

Too bad your ways bleeding outside you liars breathing.

Show me a meeting I will attend in any season.

Drop jewels around greetings build in a cipher no demons.

Calculate the numbers to a nine through the divine.

Leave the deaf dumb and blind behind my hidden lines.

Hereditary medley

Heard about the monkey hustle I spit bars off my knuckles.

Khaki flavor navy blue sport timbs like my uncle.

My day to day is between the ocean and the bay.

That is right I reside in the belly of North Cape May.

Use to give a helpful hand now I check the arm reach.

No bare feet on sand beach Sandals just sneaks.

Terrible liars playing games like hide and go seek.

Social media is an open window who need to peak.

Leave alone women with lost vibes I am chilling.

Until a DNA test result tell me I got some children.

If it is singular as if its Cingular check the carrier.

My plan is to stand and never roam outside barriers.

My atterberry roots is Carolina and elsewhere.

Wear army green apparel in the evening the loose gear.

My traits match others different sisters and brothers.

Thankful to Jackson Wiggins father of my great grandmother.

Not I

Many convos were spoken in a combo of verses.

Let us search where the earth is and get pass the curses.

Find a secret serum, cure all that has been infected.

Wipe the dust off the lessons and maybe the book answer questions.

Divided were the people of an era where i grew up.

Once again hold a cup of good luck peace to king tut.

Call upon my brethren that keep knowledge better than.

The average that lack status through my presence here is my offering.

Hit the bell as if time were cut short on a game show.

Doing things off the arm with my hand excuse my elbow.

Got to watch the faker takers when are you going to give back.

As I walk on life's tracks, I am not a well performing act.

Eyeball the poser with a higher conscious motor.

No matter the weather I keep my peace while getting older.

Say my name

Whichever one you call I respond on different levels.

My two wheels I pedal just watch how you meddle.

This ride in life exclusive no time to act foolish.

Some feel that they the coolest but they are the rudest.

My endgame to make money and handle what need be.

Work hard for my employer and keep writing poetry.

Perhaps when the time come, I will elevate and strive.

Only the real survive while the fake and phony die.

Forever gallotron and the writer king atterberry.

Legally Joel Harris but when the change come do not worry.

I am my father's dream but on a higher tier of living.

Learned to closely pay attention and fulfill the vision.

Been too long

When I step in the booth it is a portal let us explore.

They ask me to score so I give them extra raw.

Make moves without the hands-on approach I am still close.

Provide a small dose without a boast yawl do the most.

Left the old New York at the age of twenty-one.

Laid back at the shore where I can see moments come.

Exercise my mental thoughts on beaches in a county.

Never entertain the clowns underground is where you find me.

Whatever is left behind with time I am still pushing?

Set up a nice cushion I cannot be overlooking.

Hold to heart minutes and seconds clocking hours.

Manifest the power and rebuild my vessels tower.

Sensei pt.3

Only time you recognize where cowards die, new life rise.

The healthy joy surprise is presented to an eye.

What lies inside of lies the truth always produce.

Skeptical of news who really know the path of fools.

Walking thin lines of ill-mannered behavior gone.

This just another poet's poem of someone done wrong.

Hypnotic to the verbal gymnastics of mental magic.

Close doors on what is dramatic and your automatic.

Build a high intuition stand upright be persistent.

Avoid the takers while giving make better life decisions.

Open the carton of justice pour some real on the build.

With small time to kill give your will time to chill.

Hug the love!!

Come on let us enjoy what we have the time is now.

The world is so cold too many out here living foul.

Issues that are here but not addressed some careless.

How can my spirit gain rest when my living is a mess?

Got to grab the atmosphere with hands that do not fear.

Interact with the air that appear from far and near.

When they speak of men and mice is it dandruff or lice.

MUHAMMAD or Jesus Christ which one is your life.

Moments that are weird just be careful what you hear.

Let the fear disappear and be aware of those that stare.

What is written can be perceived different just open and listen.

Do not keep your mind distant just advance and be brilliant.

It is the L baby

Moving around shadow boxing the track I cannot escape it.

Some people outdated I am creative with the basic.

Return of the L ring bells on Sunday churches.

The sleepers get nervous when I am enlisted for service.

Nice bottle of brown liquor labeled on its Hennessy.

The new cannot mirror me I am an old school emcee.

What's rapper delight when you ignite flame in battle.

Make want to be tough guys fragile as if they tattled.

The hay maker book creator the poet does deliver.

Come on test my trigger touch any subject quicker.

Mind of a cyborg master my gift study the myth.

No Star Wars transform the sith into a shallow mist.

Monster drop performance kill your cadence yeah, I am ageless.

Open mazes close cages no need for me to go on stages.

If its timing forgets the shining expose the make believers.

My steez left in freezers until I slice up your pizza.

Blind eye of the law- Shanda's song

How the hell they think it is fair let me put this in the air.

There is a family out here that carry tears where is the care.

Not a jail in the world that can undo the injustice.

Put the criminal in crutches relatives still feel disgusted.

Oh, a slap on the wrist is what you get for taking life?

Maybe set him free and see him later with iron pipes.

Scenario number two build a bridge to hell fire.

Give him the needle slowly dying till his time expire.

Children with no mother how the system let them suffer.

This dark hearted brother who went out like a sucker.

Mad inside himself should have walked away for good.

Judge should have hit him hard in the face with the black book.

What happened to the sentence no such thing as repenting?

With my hand I am just lending my opinion on remembrance.

Story told of an angel so lovely, caring and giving.

The system turned a cheek and a woman who should be living.

Leave him be

If you take my lyrics, I can spin something different.

Heavy and deadly see if your spirit can really lift it.

Drop that asteroid to earth word play and box a circle.

This is not the story that you ready for so fall back turtle.

Resurrect the type of energy that was lost inside my memory.

I am all over the place writing without an itinerary.

Use to mask my emotions around clowns that be cloaking.

My meditation motion sees behind the scenes chosen.

Actors I will close your chapter presenting tables of content.

Out of seven published books search and find evidence.

He who is I another tactical brother spectacular.

What you capture does not matter I blast off like NASA.

Do you one better

No need to tweak the recipe I understand where the lessons be.

Inside myself they are telling me exploit beyond the world feed.

No host to post at many times be ghost and comatose.

Awake and hear a larger dose of knowledge from another coast.

Speak amongst some real folks the overload of leaders.

Salute the speakers educate the readers break the meters.

Access at any time abstract the mind and find the signs.

Between the lines a different kind of shine cover the spine.

Captured like a frame holding a shot taken with clear view.

Certain things in life we knew and do but cover something new.

Extravagant moments with leisure tap into the soul.

I only use the tools of goals to cereal the milk in bowls.

Me, lest & dest

Guess who has returned its the wave runner coming.

Always writing a dozen at a sixteen-bar luncheon.

Punch the world in the grill at face value what is normal.

Out of all that I been through I remain cordial.

Walk around mortal while so many out here awful.

Problems come and go just be mindful and thoughtful.

One man taught me the laws the other bout closing doors.

Together my common cause is to open my pores.

Release the dead side of my ways and pump my brakes.

When it is time to demonstrate I create and dominate.

Through my books I express the best what I profess.

Giving a shout out to my uncles it is me, lest and dest.

Not the same baby!!

They want to take away what I preserve because they heard.

Young atterberry speaking the word know who I serve.

Interplanetary supreme ruler that be the highest.

Roll around as if I am biker with them high grade tires.

My hold on my soul is greater cause I elevated.

Finally made it while yawl wasted some secrets kept sacred.

I am an underdog to favorite's written work complex and basic.

Sleep inside a dormant matrix true descendant of an ancient.

Came back inside a vessel that carried a broken anchor.

Steady moving while cruising this right here a game changer.

Exhale bangers off my mind to hand that hit paper.

Take shots with ginger-ale and face a world full of haters.

Let it go

Forget your word play I got bars for days straight off the head.

Leave you chumps left for dead check the verses i said.

Grab your pressure then apply it to the track that is playing.

I forgot what yawl saying break your silence on occasion.

Create something special on the fly with no problem.

Reemerge in Harlem feed the culture if its starving.

Turn it up if it is down spin it around underground.

Bang on clowns hit the road and head south out of town.

Close to Atlantic City sixty-five on the parkway.

Push the whip that is all white the interior is beige.

My hat blue and grey apparel burgundy and navy.

Sneakers custom made looking crazy, but it is wavy.

I am in the house

In the night life my eyes become fluorescent in the dark.

With only dim light sparked bat mode shadow a shark.

Smell whatever in the air making my senses high.

Allow my spirit guide to rise my physical THE GUARD arrived.

On any scene by any means manifest a lucid dream.

View me on a screen new technology the means.

Forward communication never hesitating population.

Through divine creation I give my own revelation.

Max build the trust of what is discussed be no rush.

Eat pizza with no crust might leave my stomach in disgust.

Crack codes of many what is scary it may vary.

Travel lite load to carry cannot afford to dilly dally.

So, I hold my transportation with steps relax with pep.

Although some forget to move ahead to see what is next.

Barricade emotions be still no time to chill and feel.

Shield any ordeal that might spill into a danger field.

Get nice

Its Friday late afternoon just got paid time to shop.

Assistance from the retailer copped something looking hot.

Beige and brown apparel looking nice for a dinner date.

Thinking of seafood and a fruit platter I do not like steak.

No potato's baked well fried fries for this guy.

For dessert she has cheesecake I will have pecan pie.

Ride the iron horse up to the Bronx on the two line.

At the house having a good time sharing a glass of wine.

Stepped out my comfort zone making out to some nice tunes.

My favorite song by the Commodores is called zoom.

Morning spin around breakfast filling the apartment.

Coffee for me and tea for her this how what start with.

Never mind you

It is a new year call it the vision time for clarity.

I am too concealed spitting the real keep your battery.

Hostile and aggressive bring your gunny I am a hitter.

Let your girl snap a picture of a cool and smooth figure.

When my pops died became the remnant of his name sake.

Broke in my grandfather pops dna and resemble his face.

Before my spirit found a vessel, I was held hostage.

Trapped inside a galaxy just to live and be modest.

Dated karma became warmer until I got in a sauna.

Met a fate had to escape before I am late like lasiandra.

Nine months later six lies and three goodbyes.

Drop the ties realized better my sight to the sky.

Capture the truth while these oodles noodle chicks get slick.

Handle my business leave the space and create the clocks tick.

No more moments of oh shit more like fuck it yeah right.

Next flight going to be to Texas sending off kites.

Let it be known pt.2

End of the day kill the story why your life so depressed.

Once upon a time you were clean now you a mess.

Checking for the old me baby girl a lost memory.

Step and let THE GUARD breathe I am outside your league.

Elevated higher than the conscious of them drinkers.

My DNA from thinkers yours probably will sink ya.

Backed by them righteous people family and friends.

You will never find again time to spend this time I win.

Will not kick the can, spin the bottle tag you it.

You act weird as if you took a wrong turn hitting a ditch.

Who I be you will never see the man behind the hands?

Drop the act close the curtain show is over to your plans.

MA.M.A.
Move against masked attitudes

Mental master still a student attending schools of power.

Praying on my knees searching for keys in god's hour.

Manifest my thoughts even in times of trouble, huddle.

Avoid strains of trouble while my brain is losing muscle.

At the water where its peace enjoying a soul retreat.

Thoughts recalibrating from the way I earn my keep.

Eyes of an old soul youthful nowadays extend the truth to.

In love with sounds so musical melodies be beautiful.

Harmony is the wave embrace all in which we live in.

No such thing as foes we all friends let it all begin.

Anytime when you are a seeker and a believer.

Here is a note to the unknown readers that feel eager.

Face it!!

Beautiful woman that I care for like no other.

Never once seen her winter mood so I call her summer.

Smile so pretty that when we talk convos get me.

Whenever she hit me pick up my jack very quickly.

We not exclusive although our feelings be elusive.

Soon as we face to face it is a no brainer conclusive.

Make the daytime jealous and the night-time admire.

Kiss her health with my fingers massage her heart that is tired.

Morally of knowing her very well and still learning.

She wears a smile that keep glowing therefor it be confirming.

Call her Sunshine because the natural side of her is true.

Only thing to do is keep her guarded fresh and new.

I am lucky

Facelift the normal forget the mask and be you.

Stand firm on your own terms watch what you choose.

Old New York former central Harlem homie.

Use to walk the streets lonely but I never been phony.

So much on my mind where is the exit so I can find.

Where do I draw the line only my mother gave me signs?

Silent whispers yes, I miss her if I can have a moment kiss her.

Give the biggest hug that is love I paint pictures.

Manipulating memories just to grow when I was young.

Who is burden of hurting release the pain to someone?

Bible page scriptures while I am drinking malt liquor.

As I think a lot quicker my heart becoming sicker.

Learned to move around energy does not matter whatever kind.

Become a go getter with the trend setters do not be blind.

Live and let live handle your biz without the tricks.

Just be mindful and thoughtful leave behind bullshit.

Step aside

Emerge from out the lair then disappear beyond your tier.

Open a twelve to those who care spit bars with hot flares.

Play a King Kong role with a Godzilla terror strike.

Use to speak the verbal's lite until I heard rappers do not write.

Ignite a buzz hard enough to shake the doubters heavy.

Been ready cracked the dam and levy throw confetti.

Congratulate the writer and reciter no ghost.

Done traveled across coast came back bringing a note.

Yeah, I am real and deadly go off on any medley.

It is the man behind the hands that jam others be jelly.

Movement be aerodynamically in-tune with god.

From a spiritual and lyrical point of view I go hard.

Where you at!

THE GUARD be at doors protecting all in vicinities.

Walk the earth with abilities do not even fuck with me.

Throw lines over heads only a few can catch it.

Sharp as razors hurt like tasers remember pages last in ages.

Trapped inside of mazes of a future that is coming.

Thought waves be running while dead minds be suffering.

One pants leg up above the timbs my hoody loose.

School these fools that keep drinking hatred juice.

Grade A attire bang the liars my conscious higher.

Lower my humbleness so I can roll like fresh tires.

Presentation accurate pen a hatchet on debaters.

Do an Ali and Frazier better grab your best trainer?

Grounds to the compound be dim when I enter.

Pick up my mail from a box that is addressed with no sender.

It is the new time but remind me of the seventies.

When my pops left my moms and got involved heavenly.

Off the arm bomb

It is the kid just respect what I spit and that is it.

Do not have me get sick and suffer with mis-forgets.

Explode without a fuse who you do not act new.

Soon cut the braids and beard bring back the old dude.

Keep the same mind frame here I come to maintain.

Strong like jack la'lanne lyrics insane and strange.

Unbearable vibes disappear when fear is near.

Catch a glance at the glare and change the whole air.

Make me want to vomit then search for verbal tonics.

Lessons from the gods hit THE GUARD like Halley comet.

A real phenomenon true to form word is bond.

No need to be alarmed I am cool and calm like the fonz.

Name not Arthur but I am an author who go to Georgia.

Next time play with water when I visit St. Pete Florida.

Never hard for me cross borders like transporters.

Spit venom unlike spider-man the transformer.

Live and direct

In the morning take a shower dress to def I profess.

Take a drive to my spot where I see what is next.

One hour before noon it is a late day for yours truly.

At the sunset beach recalibrating my energy.

As an empath I do not crash and burn with emotions.

For this life I was chosen making sure my hands Golden.

Ching Ching let it bring a nice abundance of security.

When I am feeling some kind of way the salt air heals me.

Prayers up speak to the outer world of true living existence.

For all that read or hear understand what is in my sentences.

The movement of those that keep they head on the shoulders.

I salute the team of authors that stand strong as soldiers.

GET' EM

"Gallotron Emerges Through Elevating Manifestation"

Ayo, I move amongst the snails and snakes hoping that I escape through
different doors from many halls lift the gate.

Set up bait on traps without a latch that catch whoever want to react catch
em with omnipotent facts.

Seminar attendees send me an invite so I can be wherever on the next flight
land peaceful and be alright.

Cool water rider off days of working protect my body from hurting so I
network and start preserving.

Put a shuffle on the cards in the broken dirty deck Montezuma
motherfuckers want to roll dice and get left.

Scientific mental masters with blasters peel off your plaster uncover your
sneaky ways in your laughter.

Heavy profound lyrics bend your spirit when you hear it, it is the twelve-bar
assassin do not go near him.

Who nicer than nice spank your style that's Fischer price come through like
a tonka nothing lite on the fight?

Fix the wizard with a serum of content that been abolished coming back real
solid well-polished.

Last seen the author and poet writing a magical seven between the lines
you can feel the learned lessons.

Breakdown the beautiful days allow the year of vision while sitting no
pretending playing all positions.

It is THE GUARD baby that make these waffle head haters want to ask
loose favors till I put them on an escalator.

Nowadays

Resting my physical and mental what is next to get into.

Nothing really at all there is so much that I been through.

Two marriages by law therefor I got to watch the halls.

Never placing my foot in doors that hold a past on walls.

Respect my wakeup call walk inside the planets core.

Accept my common flaws and keep up on labor laws.

Next job may hold the highest point to a degree.

I am a nine that evolve calculated off three sixty.

Even if my steps in life are broken down into portions.

My geometric make up on a square triangle talking.

Universal number with my frequency tied in.

Adapt to places I have been checking your drink if it is Island.

Eyes open wide on the ones deeply seeking.

Holding secret meetings while they plot, and they are scheming.

Want to catch this j-Dubb in a web of deception.

Until I pull, they last card with a lesson from a session.

You know what is up

The hook:

If I look just like them, talk just like them.

You know where I am from old New York, Harlem.

If I walk just like them and flick pics like them.

It is the JWA author from Harlem.

Checking temp on areas where I be found in different states.

Take me near water my aura need a break.

My whole mental state is divine whatever I find.

Go inside my mind and manifest the written lines.

Many ladders I climb, success around the corner.

She thought I was a catch turned out be a goner.

Wrong her or right her I am a writer for world muses.

No shade in my parade's provider of an exclusive.

Time sit still over the hill chill on the hurry.

My DNA atterberry so why should I worry.

Present the inevitable clarity of discussion.

If its love that is kept above, you know you got something.

Back in the central

Do not have the booth catch fire when I spark the mic wires.

What is a beat without an intro all expressed tell your messiah?

Breathe off the sleeve's tracks bleed I am underneath.

Bring a terror with these bars takeover and try to keep.

Yawl brothers still be playing this is real time finale.

For those who acting petty because your chick is caddy.

Place minds in orbit get off it never worth it.

Find a better network to service or build a surface.

The group do not decline in members we just remember.

Fuck these dumb niggas and bitches find your September.

Rock steady and hold better choices within this realm.

Knock opts off they helm until I am to watch films.

Breathe on it

Move words across margins pardon bars that spark.

The track is a go cart rolling until my voice park.

Exit off the drive perhaps I ride inside the high.

Never let my spirit die make it rise in the size.

Break bread with bakers together we do favors.

Uplift our neighbors join forces with the traders.

They got what I need and vice versa I treat.

Plant thoughts that is unique strong as a tight physique.

Levels born and gone brought back begin again.

Embracing the win-win only to feel my power spin.

Execute a play on how the wheels of life turn.

While some people live and learn it is THE GUARD that be concerned.

Time of use

My girlfriends, girlfriend is also my girlfriend.

When my lady is not around, she gifts me attention.

Speaking in tongue it is the rising of the sun.

Shining on her aura as I whisper, and she listen.

Music inside our convo as we talk about life.

Fix and eat meals that is nice without paying a price.

Even when my baby enters the door how was your day.

Those the words that I say and kiss the mouth that say okay.

The other women leave so my lady get to breathe.

Bring her back to a world that satisfy her needs.

Always I take the lead and proceed caress her face.

Make sure the love is there as we play songs by Case.

Solar roller

Elevation factors what really matter inside dark days.

Shine bright rays against skies that turn grey and stay.

Break codes of the unknown control tone as the words reach.

Tread lightly on the meek you can search find and seek.

Miraculous methods no overstepping to broad horizons.

Instead diving just swim to a moment of being sure arriving.

Justified is the eyes that show lies before the archive.

Lift the veil upon the wise and visualize with no compromise.

Tough guy facade exposed by those that know.

Ain't no telling what really show take ropes off the boat.

Got to be underneath and show a message off your chi.

Take a second just to breathe and manifest degrees.

Waves

My moves cross places of minds fueled to take off.

Typing on my acer never favor another caper.

Shots with no chaser pencil poems with no eraser.

See you suckers later read my books that hold flavor.

Moods on a grove absorb sounds through headphones.

When I am Alone morning magic set tones written in stone.

Crease on my khakis iron heat keep clothes neat.

Short sleeve button up and my Michael Jordan sneaks.

Adjust and check how I am coming going and stopping.

Facebook rocking while I am working on a doctrine.

Caterpillar pedestrian observe your ways of life.

Every day the world fight got to have wits of a knife.

Winter solstice

Trajectories on point my view of heaven in galaxies.

Apologies to honesty ways of man still bother me.

News flashing tales of what is or what's supposed to be.

Old America move around borders real life monopoly.

Starving for incentive what measures taken to help the poor.

Rowing in open water no life preserver and half ass oars.

Feelings from my core I see hidden problems at the shore.

Magnitude of mistakes as if I'm strapped in New York corner store.

Never know if the balance of right and wrong is a fifty-fifty.

Before they come and get me and lift me check how they hit me.

All because I help structure my culture along with my brothers.

We are born from out our mothers hoping that she will not suffer.

Building off the graph of our fathers that built a bridge of hope.

Cleansing the aura that was misrepresented using spiritual soap.

Mask of illusion with no intrusion the world losing.

When we start showing and proving they'll know exactly what we doing.

We in here!!

I'm sporting shades if the eyes are the window to the soul.

Keep my feelings in a mode that's cold so I don't show.

Emotions that unfold from what is told from a mole.

Student of self-control so I know which way to go.

Left the western for Eastern studies of true and living.

I can be found chilling by water spirit feel different.

Society don't listen they be forgetting about the mission.

When I expose the disposition of those snitching pay attention.

Put a dollar on the collar of dime droppers tomorrow.

You get what you pay for a hard pill to swallow.

Saluting all my brothers with prayer covers and vibes.

Extend a hand to those drowning and keep hope alive.

Hold up!!

Yawl stay hating while checking inside your mirror.

I move around that energy keeping my thoughts clearer.

Build my chi to a level where your conscious cannot go.

Taking years for it to grow time for you is just slow.

Walk amongst others that connect on higher planes.

Only reason I seem strange because I'm hip to your games.

So, it's plain to see where you be on social media.

Suffering with a fever looking and searching for a leader.

Those family and friends I be around know how I get down.

It's all love smiles and pics while yawl face frown.

Circus clown participators see you later hater.

I was born to be a cook hanging with chefs and bakers.

Play around with dough make bread and slice it properly.

There is no stopping me amazon hold my property.

Books on the shelf written by me through a moniker.

Some of my words fly over heads as if written by a foreigner.

Gardner that plant seeds of thought watch it manifest.

I only do my best to express and keep it fresh.

Back-out

This what I'm cooking in the kitchen at my table.

I'm in a spiritual trance so I'm willing and able.

I do not only write poetry books I'm from the home of spitters.

Let me sip this dark liquor no chiller get the pitcher.

Pour something cold and chase it down from the glass.

As I think about my past, I'm from a class don't ask.

Hard hitters no quitters no monkeys just gorillas.

When I was young, I saw dealers and killers in open pictures.

Hung out in the streets Harlem and Bronx with my cousins.

Think I wasn't you bugging I was always block hugging.

Show love get love talk shit and fuck chicks.

Smoking weed to the point where you got to have a roach clip.

Had they back while they hustling pockets stayed bubbling.

If I was not at my girl house cuddling, I was into something.

Never a fake brother always cool from others point of view.

Hug and pounds when I come through fuck whoever acted new.

GOODMORNING WORLD!!

ITS A BRAND NEW DAY WITH
A BRAND NEW FEELING!!

LIVE FOR TODAY NOT THE
MOMENT!!
ASE!

GOD FIRST,
EVERYTHING ELSE
IS LAST WHEN I
LAUGH!!
HA HA HA HA HA

How can I?

There's a new world happening and we
living in it.
Running on E so I can finish without
limits.
Although I'm handicap to a language that
exist.
My clarity is poor heart is rich so go and
get.
All that is available to seekers and
protectors.
Study work of tesla unofficial professor.

GOD FIRST,
EVERYTHING ELSE
IS LAST WHEN I
LAUGH!!
HA HA HA HA HA

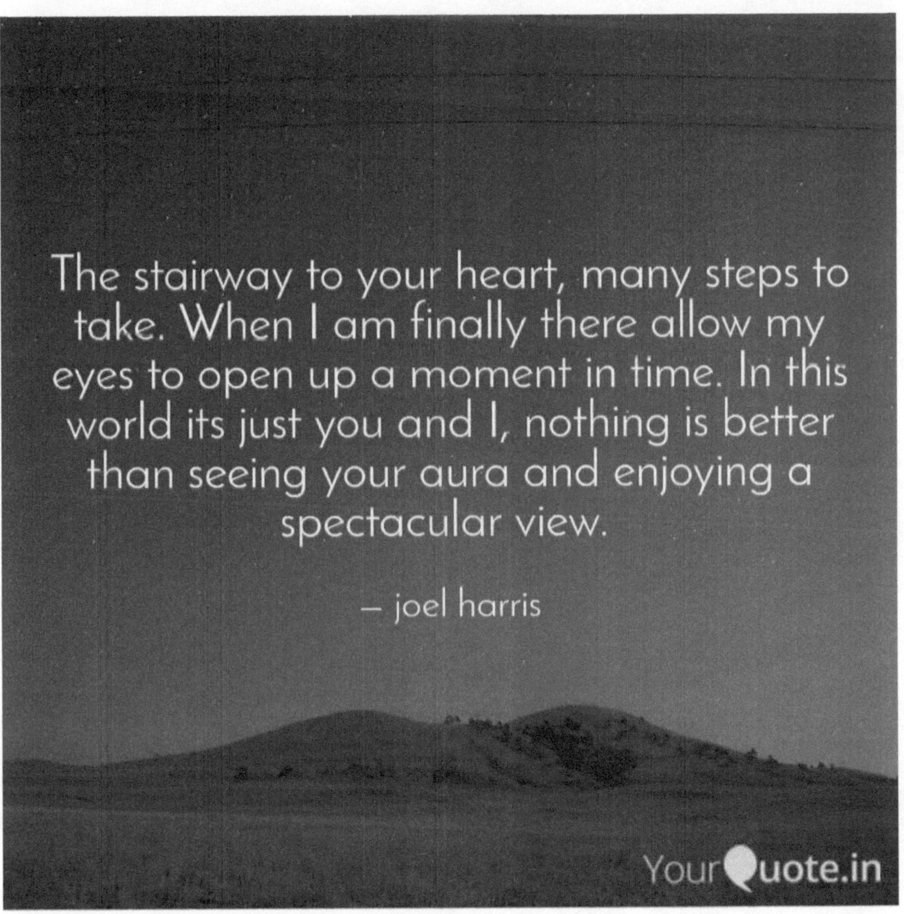
The stairway to your heart, many steps to take. When I am finally there allow my eyes to open up a moment in time. In this world its just you and I, nothing is better than seeing your aura and enjoying a spectacular view.

– joel harris

YourQuote.in

Sometimes you have to teach yourself to teach yourself.
Facts

I LOVE YOU JUST AS WELL AS
YOU LOVE ME!!
#PLEASUREPRINCIPLE
#LOVEYOURSELF

IT IS WHAT IT IS

First up
Secondly wake up
Third shake it off
Fourth take off
Five survive the ride
Six ain't shit life's a bitch

I saw you before,
but I remember
you now!

Cousin's convo

ONE THING LEARNED IS ALCOHOLICS AND CONFLICTED MINDSETS SOMETIMES RESONATE WITH THE SAME FREQUENCY AND VIBE OFF THE SAME BELIEFS.
#NOBODYISPERFECT
#SOMEBODYISONONE
#UNIVERSALLAW

i saw you before,
but i remember
you now!

REAL TALK

Baker boy with many skills still learning. Money don't move me, I move along side of the money!!!

REJUVENATION PLAN

CHECK YOUR ALIGNMENT BEFORE YOU TAKE AN
ASSIGNMENT.

MIND Of A SHEIK

MOVING LIKE The SHADOW

MY FATHERS BEST WHO ELSE

TAI CHI TRAINING RIGHT
BACK IN EFFECT LIKE IT'S
2017!!
YOU EITHER GET THERE OR
GET NO AIR!!

BORROWED TIME

Doesn't matter did it even, cant stop a man from
breathing.
I'm the fly on the wall relaxing and reading
expanding rhyme and reason.
Started off spitting bars in the halls even tagged
graffiti on walls.
whatever in life adored i have seen before and
brought it to yall.

Enter the moment abandon the
temperature, let the eyes of the sky rise
above the strength in humanity.

— joel harris

King atterberry 9

publishing

ISBN 978-0-578-23425-0

www.ingramcontent.com/pod-product-compliance
Lightning Source LLC
Chambersburg PA
CBHW031356060726

47590CB00007B/2808